The Gospel According To

DAWN

A Woman's Work of Spiritual Imagination

Dawn Annette Mills, OSB

Living Tradition Audio
Tucson, Arizona, USA

First Printing 2001
Second Printing 2005

Living Tradition Audio
P.O. Box 41312
Tucson, Arizona, USA   85717
(520) 405-0570

ISBN 0-9714807-0-2

Contents

Sunday Morning Conversation:

The Reflection Questions

Acknowledgements

This work would not have been possible without a good many people. It is important to me to acknowledge at least a few of them. I thank my mother, Dorothy Mills-Bennett, who taught me that God is real, approachable and beyond any stereotypes. I thank Jim Durkel for helping me to experience the unconditional love of God. I thank Mrs. Nicholas, my first Sunday school teacher, who taught me that imagination is holy and Sr. Matthias, an early spiritual director, who taught me to use my imagination in the prayer known as *lectio divina.*

I thank all the sisters in my religious Congregation for their help, support, and for encouraging me in the creative process. I am particularly grateful to Sisters Mary Jane, Lenora, Reparata, Sean, Valarie and Wilmarie for their assistance in bringing this project to birth. From proofreading, to fanning the flames of hope, to working the kinks out of my shoulders when I stayed at the keyboard too long, they have nurtured this work in me.

Without Mark Cesnik of Living Tradition Audio this would still be sitting in a desk drawer somewhere. His practical assistance and unflagging enthusiasm helped this word become incarnate. Bob Creager at Sound Decisions patiently listened as these stories took audio form. Marjorie Ford read the text to make sure it said what I meant.

To these and countless others who have had a hand in bringing "The Gospel According to Dawn" to life, I offer my gratitude and I pray God's blessing.

Dawn Annette Mills, OSB
July, 2001

You can hear Sister Dawn read each of these stories. Her talent as a storyteller comes through in full force in the CD and cassette editions now available.
Study groups find these recordings to be especially helpful in starting discussions of the reflection questions contained at the end of the book.
The recordings are complete and unabridged.

Living Tradition Audio
P.O. Box 41312
Tucson, AZ 85717
520-405-0570
www.LivingTraditionAudio.com

Sister Dawn's work also available at
www.BenedictineSisters.org

Introduction

This book was first conceived July of 1979 during a retreat. I was praying over the temptations of Christ in the wilderness from Luke's Gospel, when all of a sudden I noticed that my imagination had turned a corner. I was experiencing the story from a completely different point of view. I was listening to it as if Jesus were explaining what had happened to him, and as if he were sharing his experience with someone who would understand.

I carried that meditation with me for five years, pondering it in my heart. Finally, I knew I had to put it down on paper. The story "Home Coming" was born. I had no idea at that point that others would follow, but as they did I wrote them down. At some point, I realized that I was writing my own gospel. So I opened up my imagination and these stories flowed into existence.

This gospel is imaginary.

The stories are based on the originals found in Matthew, Mark, Luke, and John, but this is a gospel according to Dawn. My own experiences, meditations, dreams and other personal realities have infiltrated the original stories and transformed them into what is here.

My gospel is a view from a different angle. I've gone behind the scenes, between the lines, checking up on people twenty years later. In doing this I've allowed some unknown characters to emerge and some previously know characters to change radically.

The resulting stories may be surprising for some. For readers who have a very literal understanding of Sacred Scripture some of these portrayals may even come as a shock.

At no time have I held the stories irreverently. I have too much respect for the Gospels of Jesus. Indeed, these imaginative stories were born from almost twenty years of daily praying with the Bible and trying to put it into practice.

It was in doing spiritual direction with others that I came to realize how many people have difficulty relating the Biblical stories to their own lives. Messy human feelings aren't always recognizable in the way we have been trained to approach Scripture. The humanity that is visible in the Bible is almost completely invisible by the time we experience it in liturgies.

That is why I have recommended to my directees and retreatants to try to practice reading the Bible from the inside and the outside. By that I mean I encourage them to first try to enter into the Bible passage with their imaginations, and to simply be present to the scene as vividly as possible. That is the process that actually birthed these stories in me.

Secondly, I recommend that the person praying with Scripture then let the passage get inside them. Where has this dynamic really happened in their own life story? It was this process that gave rise to the reflection questions that I have included in the final section of this book. In this gospel I have particularly highlighted the feelings, the movements and the humanity of my characters. I confess that they are all me. Perhaps the reader will also recognize a few of the faces presented here.

I have emphasized women in my gospel. This was done, mainly, because I am a woman. I feel at home with these stories, they reflect my own feelings and experiences. No doubt the men in my stories reflect that, too.

In the process of writing these reflections, I found myself writing a feminine gospel to deal with the experiences and values of women, especially women who may not have had a voice in other writings.

This is an imaginary gospel. It is my hope that the Holy Spirit has had something to do with it, but I accept the responsibility for forming these words and images.

They are born from hours of prayer and hours of active imagination. Thus the more vividly they can be imagined, seen, heard and felt, the more the meaning will be revealed. They are especially written to be read out loud. Ultimately they are meant to be prayed.

To assist the reader in praying these stories I have listed the Biblical references for each in the final chapter. Along with Biblical citations I have included some reflection questions based on each story.

I hope the reader will find them to be a springboard for praying these stories into the framework of real daily life. The stories themselves contain many questions, some of which I am still asking.

My God, it seems, enjoys questions. This gospel came as part of the answer.

May God speak the Word through it.

The
Innkeeper's
Wife

"Who had time for stargazing? I was cooking for half of Bethlehem..."

The streets were crowded with people. Rich people, poor people, dusty and dirty people, the beggars came from all corners. The bewildered, tired, weary travelers were banging on the doors looking for someplace to stay. Old Augustus had no idea what he was doing to a place like Bethlehem when he issued that decree. I tell you, it will cost more in taxes to enforce it than will ever be collected. So much for Roman Law!

With all that going on, how was I supposed to notice them? How was I to tell them apart from the rest of the crowd? Yes, I know, she was pregnant, but I didn't know she was that pregnant! What was that man of hers thinking to bring a woman in her condition along on such a journey? I swear some men have no sense. Though I can tell you that quite a few brought families along. We had so many little ones running around, the yard looked like a festival. And every one of them was in a dozen places at once, and in at least eleven places they shouldn't be! I know that several of the women staying here were in a family way. What was I supposed to do with another one? We'd already taken in ten more people than we had room for to begin with.

When the common room had no more space for bedding on the floor, we started pointing to the stable. I guess that's where they must have gone in the end. I didn't know anything was going on until the hill folk came in to us. As if I didn't have enough to take care of with people, they came complete with sheep. Can you imagine it?

No, I didn't see any stars that night. Who had time for stargazing? I was cooking for half of Bethlehem, at least by the feel of it. But the hill folk did look a little star-struck. Then that tale of angels! No, I don't know what to make of it. All I heard that evening was the banging of pots and pans, the cries of the children and the laughter of the men after drinking too much wine. Who had ears for angels?

Besides, surely the Holy One of God would not be born in a cave, at least not a cave behind my house, anyway! Such tales are just stories for children and old men and dreamers. Aren't they? I don't know what people are saying. But if the messiah was born that night, and at a time like this, all I can say is God save us!

Home Coming

What had happened to her son? It was her son. Yes, that was plain. Yet, somehow he was no longer hers alone.

The sun hung low in the sky. Evening was fast approaching. Something had prompted her to add a little more to the pot for supper, even more than a little more. He had been gone for forty days, he would be hungry. And something told her he would be home tonight.

The neighbors still whispered gossip as they passed the house. Where had he gone, and why? It had happened all so suddenly. He had seemed such a stable man, fine and upstanding, a good worker, yes, and a skilled craftsman. True, he was a little old to be living in his mother's house, without a wife to settle him. But until the Jordan prophet had come along no one really thought it strange. Then all at once the prophet preached and off the carpenter had gone, God knew where. Just like a love struck boy, or a moon struck puppy. He'd left his work unfinished and his mother to fend for herself. It was a crime. There is the commandment to honor one's parents. Had he no fear of God?

She'd heard it all, the half spoken complaints and the gossip, but she simply smiled them away. He hadn't run off. She knew him well enough.

If he was running it was because he was being called, and the direction of his footsteps led onward, not away. When the prophet had come to the Jordan her son's eyes had blazed with questions.

They reminded her of thoughts that she had pondered long ago. Tonight she had sense of learning an answer or two. She wondered, though, if she really wanted to know the answers after all.

She had learned to ponder as she moved through life, and her movements tonight were in the direction of welcome. The house was clean and the floor was swept. Extra water was kept cool in the shadows of the inner wall. The cooking fire outside the door proclaimed a simple, hearty meal for a hungry wandering son.

Then from a chest of hand-carved wood she drew a garment, white and soft, woven and without a seam. A welcome gift, a parting gift, a remembrance of angels and of her. No sooner had she laid it out, than she felt his shadow on her shoulder. Turning slowly, not to rush the mystery, she faced him and his smile.

What had happened to her son? It was her son, yes, that was plain. Yet, somehow he was no longer hers alone. His eyes still flickered with the fire of burning bushes on mountain heights. His lips still smoldered where purifying coals had kissed his mouth with the words of God.

This man had walked with angels. This man had faced his God.

How does a mother deal with a prophet in his own native place? How does she deal with immanent majesty? Having learned the lesson from ancient eastern kings, with serene composure she said, "the water's in there." Her head was pointing the direction as she handed her guest the prophet's robe that she had wrought with painstaking care.

"Supper will be ready soon. When you've washed I'll comb your hair."

Why had she said that? Wasn't he old enough to do such things for himself? He was a man before God, a prophet. But tonight he was still her son, her little boy grown up, and she wanted to be sure that the light encircling his face wouldn't burn her hands.

In a few moments he stood before her again. It seemed as if, with all that solitude behind him, he did not want to be alone. He pulled a cushion up before her and sat almost in her lap. The new, white wool robe spun fine and soft caressed them both in tenderness. The water still dripped from the dark curls of his hair, running down his beard to the collar of his robe, like some ancient priest's anointing.

The comb was close at hand; as if it knew it would be needed soon. Forty days of tangles from the breath of God and Elijah's wind had made a knot of raven hair. It would take time to untangle it. Supper could wait till this ministry was done. She did it slowly, with gentleness, the way she'd combed a baby's hair so many years ago. The tender tugging of the comb seemed to bring him comfort.

He looked less like a Moses now and more like her only son, till she caught he eye still blazing. The muscles of his shoulders felt strong against her knees. What burdens had they been shaped to carry? She wasn't sure she wanted to know. She knew she needed to ask. "Tell me what happened."

He drew her arms around his shoulders and held them there in silence. When he finally spoke he asked her a question that answered everything. "Imma, what do you think the Messiah will be like?"

The silence lasted just long enough for her to find the comb again. She knew his questions far too well to make a hasty answer. He turned around and gazed at her with a look so full of love it might have been enough even if it were the last. "You tell me," the mother in her said.

He told her then his story of Jordan prophets fulfilling the law and calling down thunder that fell on his ear like the cooing of a dove, a sound that felt like comfort while rocking his heart with power.

She sensed the soul within him stir igniting his own inner strength to challenge the desert places. She saw the wild animals walking in his memory, now threatening, now consoling, being always what they were meant to be.

She felt the shade that had tried to darken his resolve with thoughts unworthy of a prophet. He had been tempted to be other than what he was born to be.

"If only I were another Moses." He confided how he had thought of bringing manna to a people who hungered for the Lord. Perhaps if he opened their mouths with bread they could be filled with God. But the day of Moses had come and gone. The people hungered for freedom and life. God didn't need another Moses now.

"If only I were David." His inner eye gazed at ancient kingdoms filled with the glory of God and His Anointed. A king could lead the people to a kingdom of God, if he ruled with justice and preserved the land in peace. But David had been a warrior king, and Rome was not Philistia. How could a king in this day and age be a messianic prince of peace?

"If only I were God." Through him she felt the desert shake with thunder, fire and cloud, not in the sense of reprimand, but with anticipation. He was so close to the Father's plan, but was this his Father's way? She knew that being God might be well within his grasp, but grasping it, in power and might, would make him less than God. How close the shadowed one had come to laying low the Father's plan of mingling divinity with human flesh and blood!

"I can only be myself," his voice was soft with reverence. He knew what God had done for him, step by step since before the world began. He had come to fulfill that ancient will in a way that was his alone.

She had a sense of what he meant. Hadn't she said something similar once? God would be given to those hungry enough. Life would rule in the realm of death. The ancient will, with human help, would be done.

In the morning she knew he would leave again. She would be left alone in waiting. But this time she would follow him and be there at his side. She knew where she would find him, in the midst of the crowds, on the roads to Jerusalem, in the recesses of her heart which the prophet had warned her would be pierced by a sword.

Not that long ago an angel voice had asked her if she would consent to a love that would bear with all of this. She'd been so young, so very naïve. Still the yes of that moment rang strong tonight.

She stood on almost steady legs and went to bring the supper in, to share it with the prophet, the messiah son who sat on the floor.

For forty days he'd hungered, but it wasn't for this kind of food. She knew that God had fed him well on spirit and fire before letting him wander home. Now her son would eat supper readily enough from wooden bowls carved with care.

Tonight was the night of journey bread and communion meals, of sacrifice and praise.

Woman Healed

She had given up hope. Almost.

The crowds surged around like waves on the shore. He stood like a rock in their midst. The force of the people breaking upon him and ebbing away. She needed to touch him. That's all, just touch him. To clasp his hand, to brush his fingers, to hold even the tassel of his robe, the hem of his garment. She needed only to touch him. She knew it. But the crowds flowed around him like water and she felt swept out to sea.

For twelve years she had suffered. The loss of blood, the loss of strength, even the loss of her place among her people. She was unclean, outcast.

Even to be pushing through this crowd was a sin for her. She was supposed to stay away, to protect good people from contamination. What would they say if they found her among them? An unclean woman who bleeds.

It wasn't as if she hadn't tried to find a cure. God alone knew how hard she'd tried, how far she sought, to what lengths she had gone, to no avail. She had left her home. She had spent her fortune, her family inheritance. She had risked her remaining strength experimenting with exotic cures. She had given up hope. Almost.

Then she heard of a demon cast out, a fever rebuked, a leper cured. There was a story of a paralytic who now walked. There were even rumors that the dead had been raised. All this at the word of an itinerant preacher, the Nazareth rabbi. Some even said he was the messiah of God. That he had power so many could witness. He was her last hope of healing; she had to believe.

She believed enough to risk the crowds, to risk the revelation of her shame. She needed to touch him. She had made that her goal. It gave her the strength to struggle through the mass of people before her and stretch out her hand to the hem of his robe.

Everything stopped as the lightning surged through her. From the soles of her feet to the hair of her head she felt the echo of power. Then her womb, source of her suffering, began to pulse with a friendly warmth. She knew that she'd been healed.

Then he spoke, not with rage but with wonder, wanting to know where his power had gone. Who had touched him, had triggered his caring? Who had needed him? He searched all around.

His followers told him he must be mistaken, many had touched him. They didn't understand. But she knew he was looking, he needed to find her. With health pulsing within her she knelt at his feet.

He smiled. His eyes danced and his whole body smiled. He saw her whole and healed. He understood how she came to be that way, now he wanted to know why.

As he reached out his hand, he nodded the question, his eyes wide with wondering. She started to speak.

She told him her story, of her sickness and suffering. Braving the people's disgust at her disease, she admitted it. Vindicated by her hope in him she confided that too.

Not certain what awaited her, but trusting what had happened in her, she owed him her truth and she spoke it.

He looked at his followers. They looked at the ground, or the sky, or the crowd. They knew he knew better than they. He knew they had learned a lesson in listening to him.

He looked at her and blessed her, lifting her up to go on her way. Then he turned with the tide of the crowd and went with his people to the healing needed in Jairus' house.

Talitha Cumi

"I woke up hungry.

His voice made me hungry."

"Talitha cumi! Talitha cumi!"

Little girl, get up!

Such simple words, such a friendly voice. How could I possibly resist? I couldn't, of course, and I didn't. I simply got up. Actually, I woke up laughing. My mother and father both had tears running down their faces. Their cheeks were wet as they embraced me. I remember it all so clearly. But then, you know the story or you wouldn't be here talking to me.

What was it like to be "dead" and then come back? Well, it's very hard to explain. While I was surely somewhere, it wasn't a place that fits our words or ideas. It was a place of light. I was surrounded by happiness and acceptance and love. I thought I heard my mother's mother singing my favorite song. I may have only dreamed that, though. Sometimes, now, it's hard to tell. It seems to me that there were some "ones" with me and more coming to meet me, as though they'd been waiting for me to arrive.

It was a wonderful experience. I wasn't in a hurry to be gone from there, I can tell you that. I know, too, I won't mind going back.

Then why did I return here? Well. He called me. A voice as bright as the light before me and as soft as the love that surrounded me. His voice had the depth of thunder and the gentleness of snow. He called me. It was a profound moment, raising the dead. It was also as simple as calling a little girl to get up. I woke as naturally as if I'd only overslept past breakfast time.

His voice said, "Rise and partake. Bring forth fruit, bear children, love families, give comfort, live long in the land and dwell secure." That's what I heard in his voice. His words, on the other hand, were only coaxing a little sleepy head. His words roused a sleeping body. His voice stirred a latent heart.

I woke up hungry. His voice made me hungry. I hungered for the love of a husband and family. I hungered for an opportunity to care for my parents in their old age. I hungered for time to feed the hungry, clothe the naked and heal a broken heart or two.

I hungered to hear other words spoken by the voice that called me home.

I hungered and so I woke. He told them to give me something to eat. So, I took a bite out of life. I have tasted the joys and sorrows of living.

30

I've savored the delight of being loved and of loving. I must say that I've been more than satisfied.

I'm hungry now for only one more thing. I hunger to hear his voice again. I listen, always, to hear "talitha cumi" that will wake me to life again.

The Adulterous Woman:

One Woman's Opinion

"What was that about 'whoever is without sin'? I'm without the sin of adultery!"

It's about time she was caught at it! What I don't understand is why they didn't go ahead and stone her. It's the Law! She was taken in the act. God knows how guilty the harlot is. She betrayed her husband, her marriage bed, all for her own pleasure. I heard she was caught with her husband's steward. The one person the old man trusted!

And you can't blame the steward, after all, how could he say no? You know the story of Joseph and Potiphar's wife. Well, we've seen it again today!

The nerve of that rabbi. Why did they ask him anyway? It isn't as if the scribes really believe in him you know. No, I'm sure they thought to trap him. But they didn't. Oh, he didn't say a thing against the Law, or a thing about that woman. They didn't get a word to use against him. But they had something to use against her! She was caught in the act I tell you.

So why did they let her go? Why didn't they press that rabbi about her, about her sin of adultery? Then they might have been able to stone them both.

What was that about "whoever is without sin"? I'm without the sin of adultery. I may have forgotten to wash my hands. I may have failed to pay a few coppers to the Temple. But I'm a God fearing woman. I haven't broken any of the great commandments. And I'm just a woman!

You can't tell me that these holy men, these scribes and Pharisees, aren't at least as pious as I am. I won't believe that one of them couldn't have cleared his conscience enough to just get it all started.

Of course I couldn't throw the first stone. Not me! I mean, if they, if those religious men couldn't do it, what would it look like if I did? What would people think?

I'll bet not one of them would have understood my zeal for the Law. Everyone knows that I haven't been on the best of terms with that woman. Not that I regret that for one moment. Who would want a good relationship with an adulteress? But, you know how people talk.

Besides, just you wait. It isn't over yet. She has her husband to face and her father. She won't have the arms of the steward waiting to protect her anymore, either. And she still has to live here. Maybe justice wasn't done according to the Law, but she won't find things quite the way they were. There will be retribution yet.

That rabbi may forgive, the scribes may pardon her, the Pharisees may even walk away, but God knows, she still has to live with us.

A Neighbor's View

"It's true, she broke the Law, but … It seems to me she was sinned against, too."

I think you're being far too hard on her. I feel sorry for the girl. She is barely more than a girl you know. I think she's had it hard enough. Her father should've known better than to marry her off to a man twice her age.

I know, Isaac is a good man. It's not his fault that his dear Deborah died and left him alone. But I'm sure that's been part of the problem. Isaac never stopped grieving his first wife, and he hasn't made a place in his life for a new one. She, on the other hand, is young. She needs a man's love.

No, I'm not justifying what she did. I don't condone it. Yes, it's against the Law, you're right. I don't approve either, but I do understand. Isaac was living in a world of his own, a world where Deborah was still with him. He gave this girl every material thing she could want, his wealth afforded them both that. But, that isn't enough for a young bride! I'm not so old yet that I can't remember what it was like to be young.

It's no wonder really, with Isaac so distant from her, she was bound to turn to someone.

Why not his steward? He was home more often than Isaac. She had more company with him, more security in some ways than she had from her husband. You have to admit he isn't hard to look at either. He is more her own age, more her temperament.

Really, he's more the kind of man her father should have found for his daughter in the first place. Only he cared more about the money than he did for his daughter.

It's true, she broke the Law, but I don't think she was the only sinner involved. It seems to me she was sinned against, too. And I feel sorry for her.

As for those precious holy men, it seems to me that if everyone knew about this harlot wife of Isaac's, they certainly took their time in doing something about it. It doesn't seem to me that anyone thought it was important at all until this rabbi appeared. Then all of a sudden we have an adulteress in our midst and a legal question for the scribes.

I think the rabbi had the right of it. There was more sin to look at here than just hers. I'm not sure there were enough stones in the fields for all the sinners there. Maybe you have only a few petty faults, but in my heart I didn't have the strength to lift a pebble against her. And let me tell you right now that I won't be lifting my hand against her in the future either!

You're right, she does have a husband to face, and I hope this wakes him from his grief and makes a husband of him. I hope this makes her father wiser with his other daughters as well. And as for neighbors, I intend to be just that to her. I will not raise my hand, not use my tongue against her. If I didn't condemn her in public it would be false witness to do so now. That is against the commandments too, you know.

She sinned. I've sinned too, though maybe not quite so publicly. But no one has ever forgiven me quite so publicly either.

The Other Man

"…Think about it. You can't take one person in the act of adultery."

Think about it. You can't take one person in the act of adultery. It isn't a crime you can commit alone. It wasn't something she could do by herself. Her lover should have been there. But when they came charging into the chamber, they didn't want me, just her.

I should have been taken. She shouldn't have had to stand there alone with no one to protect her, no one to speak for her. No one was there to shield her from their eyes or from the stones. I should have been there, but they didn't want me. They didn't take me, and I was too afraid to go by myself.

She wasn't a whore or a harlot. She was a young woman, a lonely woman, full of life and beauty and grace. She was warm and bright and so lovely, and she was married to a man who couldn't have cared less.

He bought her things, toys, jewels, diversions. You can't divert a woman like her from living, from life itself. She was too warm to be kept alive by cold things. And he was away so much of the time.

He told me to look after her. He practically threw her into my arms. He should have... He should've been able to trust me. I should've remembered my place. I should've been more careful in our meetings. I could have kept us both from the temptation of sin. I should have known we'd be discovered, that he would be hurt, that she could be destroyed. I should have... I should have been taken with her. I should have gone with her to die.

God in heaven forgive her, forgive us both. We have sinned, transgressed, committed adultery. But, we have also loved. Loving can't be a sin, can it? But loving wasn't for us, not with Isaac and a covenant between us. We knew it too. But it didn't stop us. We didn't stop to think to consider, or even pray until..., until too late.

So what's there to say? Preserve us from temptation? Preserve her from condemnation? Preserve her from the stones? Lord, God, preserve her from being alone. After all, adultery isn't a sin you can commit alone. You can't do it by yourself.

In adultery, always, more than one person, more than one woman, more than just one must be guilty.

The Question

"…they'd have to be pretty serious sins to intimidate that crowd."

What did he write in the sand? That's what I've been asking everybody. I was too far back to see. The scribes and Pharisees were in the way. Too big a crowd had gathered. Even those up close haven't answered my question.

Everybody saw him writing, or at least tracing, in the sand. But nobody knows what it was. Everyone remembers what he said. Everyone remembers what that girl looked like, standing in front of the crowd with less dignity than a slave in the market. They made her stand there, you know, for everyone to stare at and ridicule. I thought she was going to tremble to death before the stoning ever started.

Everybody remembers watching the rabbi bend down to the ground. He turned his back to her, did you notice that? He turned his back, but it didn't seem like rejection, it was as if he were refusing to stare at her. It was as if his back was the only privacy he could give her. Anyway, he turned his back and bent down to draw something on the ground. Then, when the holy men finally pressed him for his judgement, he said that business about casting the first stone.

Then he bent to writing again. That same tracing, what was it?

Was it just some meaningless busy work? Was he trying to insult the scribes by showing them that he had no more concern for their judgements than a child playing in the dirt? I overheard one old woman say she believed he had written the sins of the scribes and Pharisees right there in plain sight, so they couldn't pretend they were sinless. If that's true, it would explain why no one who could see would tell me what he wrote. Who would admit to their sins right there in front of God and everyone? But, it's pretty hard to believe that one rabbi would know the sins of all those men. I mean, they'd have to be pretty serious sins to intimidate that crowd. Then again, maybe not. Maybe they'd only have to be the sins that nag at any human heart, the secret thoughts we don't act upon, but only want to do.

Still how would the rabbi know which sins to write? Or is that the trick? After all, don't we all have the same demons to fight? Don't we all have the same commandments to guide us because we all have the same temptations to mislead us? Is adultery beyond any of us, especially adultery of the heart?

Was it a miracle that we witnessed today? I know we saw forgiveness, but I'm talking about the miracle of conviction. Not the conviction of a criminal taken in adultery, but the conviction of holy people caught in their unholiness. The miracle isn't that the rabbi knew the sins of the Pharisees, but that the Pharisees knew their own sins when they saw them on the ground. They knew their own sins and admitted them, at least to themselves. Perhaps by not throwing stones they admitted their sins to us as well. Isn't that a miracle!

Then again, maybe the rabbi wrote nothing on the ground. Or maybe he wrote our virtues, or even the virtues of the woman behind him. Maybe he wrote the commandments to remind us of more than just the sixth or the ninth. Maybe he wrote what each one of us needed to have him write. Maybe he only seemed to be writing on the ground, maybe he was really writing in the hearts of each of us who saw him. Maybe he writing that he forgives us too. Maybe we all stood convicted today, but the miracle was that no one was condemned.

She Who Loved Much

"Love had meant a denarius for a good night's work."

I'm not sure why I did it. I guess it sounds a little strange when I tell it like this. But I didn't stop to think about it then. It was just something I had to do. If I had thought about it, I don't think I'd have had the nerve.

What surprises me is the way I can remember all of the little details now, even though I wasn't really aware of the details then. The house was very nice. Simon, you must know, is very much a man of means. To listen to him talk you'd think he was a priest or Levite, but he's really a Pharisee who deals in the trade of olive oil. It must bring quite a profit by the looks of his house.

The night of the banquet the table was covered with spotless white linen. The coverings of rich embroidery and shimmering silks on the couches looked imported from the East. The colors were brilliant. I remember the rabbi reclined on a couch covered with blues and greens. The colors were vibrant, like afternoon sky and morning grass. It seemed so appropriate for him. His robe looked so white against the colors of the couch.

When I came in, the servants were presenting the guests platters of dates and soft white cheese, dried figs and sliced apples and light white wines. The main dishes had been removed already. I'd waited to enter his presence. I'd hoped to come in when the entertainment had attracted everyone's attention. That way I wouldn't draw so much attention to myself. I'd heard the musicians begin to play before I entered the room. There was a mellow sound of reeds and strings. Simon was telling stories of caravans and olive trade.

I made my way to the foot of the rabbi's couch. He gave me only the barest glance, but his eyes held a glint of welcome. I knew he recognized me. I thought of the way he'd smiled at me that day in the crowd. When others were vying to even touch his cloak, he'd made it a point to take my hand. No man had ever touched me that way before. It wasn't my hand he had in his clasp. He was touching my heart.

It's hard to talk about it. I don't have words even for myself. I think of the way I felt that day and the only word that comes to mind is love. But at that time in my life, love was a word I'd heard too often, and it didn't mean the same thing at all. Love had meant a denarius for a good night's work. I've been looking for a word that means belonging, but also means being free. A word that means he knows me and still won't turn me away. I wanted a word similar to love, meaning not the heat of bodies but the warmth of souls. Have you ever heard of friendship at first sight? That's the way I thought of it, I fell in friendship with him. So it didn't seem so strange at all, once I knew that he would be at Simon's house. I had to go and see him.

I told you I stood behind his couch. I knelt on the floor at his feet. I don't really know what I'd planned to do.

I had some perfume, from a caravan guide who once liked the way I treated him. It was expensive perfume, exotic, scented with flowers I can't even imagine. It was exquisite perfume, too rich for me. I'd been saving it for an occasion that never seemed to come.

I'd brought it to the banquet as a gift. I thought the rabbi could sell it to meet his needs. He could give the money to the poor if he wanted. Or defray his own expenses as he traveled from town to town. That was my original intention.

But as I sat beside his feet, something shifted deep inside. I touched his feet almost to assure myself that this moment was real.

I cried. I don't know why exactly. I hadn't cried for years on end, not for the pain, or the loss, or the fear. Not for the shame and ridicule. Not even for my sins. I cried because he knew me for what I was and he didn't send me away. I felt grateful. I felt forgiven. I felt accepted and my only response was tears.

I never knew I could cry so much. His feet were wet when I saw them again. I dried them with my hair. Ever since I was a little girl my hair has been my glory. Strangers used to stop and say how beautiful it was. No mantle I owned would hide it, no veil could compare in worth. It was the best I had. I could offer nothing else to the man who had given me back my self.

I'm not sure what moved me then to anoint his feet with the perfume. I think it was my way of saying thank you. He had walked so gently through the paths of my life. I felt him walk with me the day he took my hand. He knew the places of my darkness. He knew where I'd been. Still, he reverenced me in the journey.

He offered me a resting-place, and as we rested together I rubbed his feet softening the calluses with my fragrant oil. I even bent and kissed his feet. I sensed they would travel other paths where he would walk alone.

Somewhere in all this I began to realize that every eye was turned on me. I was ashamed, for a moment, of all the attention I had attracted. Do you find it hard to believe I'd really forgotten the crowd in the room with us? It is hard to believe, unless you've felt his presence and know the power he commands.

You should have heard him telling Simon I was making up for what Simon's hospitality lacked. I didn't understand at first, but it seems that the rabbi really hadn't been so welcome here. He said that he hadn't found an open heart until I had come into the room.

Simon just looked with that look I recognized. He'd heard of me before. He knew me by reputation, and what he'd heard wasn't good. The Pharisees at table were repelled by the presence of a woman like me, anyway those who weren't amused.

The rabbi told them I shouldn't be judged. He told them that love is a sign of forgiveness. He told me to go in peace, and I've been peaceful ever since.

I don't want that to sound naïve. Life still has its ups and downs. That banquet was a turning point. It turned my life around.

You know I'm working with the weavers now. I love to work with blues and greens in memory of him. And a widow with an empty nest made room in her home for me. Even respectable women smile at me now when we meet. So much has changed.

But the biggest difference has been in my understanding of love. I used to give myself to others to take my loneliness away. Now I see that I wasn't really giving anything at all. I was trying to fill an emptiness with air, a basket with water. I sometimes think that love isn't something we can give at all. I know it certainly can't be bought or sold. Love, I think, is only something we can be.

The rabbi who touched my soul. Whose feet I touched in Simon's house. The one I fell in friendship with. He'd understand, I'm sure. The real sign as to how I've changed is how I'm loving you.

The Widow
of Naim

*"My first born son...
my only child is
dead.*

*Can you, all knowing
God, ever know what
that means?"*

Listen to them. Listen to the wailing. All day these women have wailed, all day these men have mourned with me. Lord God, do you hear it? Do you hear our grief? Do you hear my grief? Do you hear my tears for my son, my only son whom I have loved?

The Lord gives, the Lord takes away, blessed be the name of the Lord. That's what they say to me. To me, a widow these last fifteen years, to me who yesterday was a mother in Israel and who now has no one.

The Lord gives, the Lord takes away, where is the blessing? Wouldn't it have been better not to have received at all? Blessed are those who are barren, blessed are the women whose wombs never bore, whose breasts never gave suck! Blessed... Blessed is the name of the Lord.

Lord, why did this happen to us? Wasn't Jacob enough? Wasn't my husband, Jacob, enough of a loss to bear? Why now my son, my only son? He was all I had!

Lord it's hard to be a woman. It's harder still to be a widow, to lose the companion of my life.

He was such a good man, so gentle. He loved this world, he loved his work, he loved his son, and he loved me. And I love him, too. Then he died. And I mourned. And I let him go, because I had a son to raise, our only son.

My son was also quite a man, so like his father. Joshua was so good when Jacob died. He never complained. He grew up so fast, too fast perhaps. His father would have been so proud of the way he took over the business, the way he took his place in the synagogue, the way he took care of his mother.

A young man wants to make his own way and live his own life; a widowed mother isn't an easy burden for a man ready to make a home for himself. Lord, can you understand what it's like for a young man to have a widowed mother on his hands. My son was good to care for me, to keep the law, to love me.

Would I have done so well given the same choice? Would you have done so well? How do you treat this widow? Lord, do you understand?

It hurts to be alone, to lose the ones you love. It hurts to be a widow and lose my only son. I need to know you understand, that you will have pity on me! Will you console your handmaid in her grief?

Soon they'll come and bury him. The earth will be his home. My home will be empty and I'll be all alone. How could you do this? I don't understand! Do you see our sufferings? Do you hear our cries? Listen to the wailing! He was so young, so good. Lord, why?

Is death the price of sin? Is this some holy justice? What fault or sin did you find in us? I will know that at least. Or is death something other than the debt of sin? Is death something that even causes you grief? Lord God, enthroned on the praises of Israel, do you take my son in justice? Or do you receive my son with tears on your cheeks?

I believe in your mercy. Could I talk this way if I didn't? Even when I cry in pain, it's your shoulder that I cry on. My first born son, my faithful one, my only child is dead. Can you, all knowing God, ever know what that means? But even if you understood, what good is that to me? The gates of death are closed and locked. My son will not come back to me.

Be merciful, then, in the time that's left to me. Bring me soon to those I love. Lord, pretend you have an only son. Imagine the pain of separation, the grief that dying leaves behind. Then Lord, do for mine what you would do for him. Or if you had a mother, a widow all alone, then pity me with filial love that I can understand. You were a friend to Abraham and gave his Isaac back to him. Yet, David lost his Absalom, and you loved David too. But these were men and I am me, and you are God above all this. I need to believe, or at least pretend, that you understand, and can feel as I do.

No, not yet, it can't be time. Lord, help me on this last long walk to give my son into your hands. It hurts so much, how can I stand and walk? Lord, do you have an idea what this pain is like? It's a sword that pierces a mother's heart! I do believe you know what it's like. I must believe. But I do not understand.

Jesus went to a town called Naim, and his disciples and a large crowd accompanied him. As he approached the gate of the town a dead man was being carried out, the only son of a widowed mother. A considerable crowd of townsfolk were with her. The Lord was moved with pity upon seeing her and said to her, "Do not cry." Then he stepped forward and touched the litter; at this the bearers halted. He said, "Young man, I bid you get up." The dead man sat up and began to speak. Then Jesus gave him back to his mother. [Luke 7:11-15*]

*The Jerusalem Bible, Alexander Jones, ed., Doubleday & Co., Inc. Garden City, NY 1966.

The Widow's Mite

"I know it's a pretty pitiful offering. But, you know, it's also everything."

Lord, God, King of the Universe! Only you could do this for me. You have been merciful to me again. My life is restored from the pit. My spirit rejoices and my soul is glad. A part of me that I thought was dead has been reborn. Something that I'd thought long withered has blossomed. Thank you!

What return can I make to the Lord for his goodness to me? The psalmist said, "I will make a sacrifice of praise." That's what I want to do. I want to make an offering, a thanksgiving sacrifice to the Lord who has given me so much to be thankful for. But how? Lord knows I've a good intention, but that's not the same as a ram, a lamb or even a couple of pigeons. Lord, you know how the priest would laugh at me. Not that I mind the laughing, it might do them some good to laugh, but I'm sorry to have so little to give.

Two copper coins. They're not much, are they? What can even you do with two copper coins? They won't add much to the glory of your house. They won't add much profit to your Temple servants. But it's up to you to use them as you please. Perhaps some orphan will have some bread through these alms. Or maybe with enough copper coins a vestment will be finished to add a bit of glory to the Holy Days. Two copper coins. I know it's a pretty pitiful offering. But, you know, it's also everything.

Two copper coins. It is a sacrifice, for me. Lord, I offer you the food I won't buy, the wood I can't afford, the cloth I'd like to have. Lord, I won't bring you the life blood of one of your little creatures. No, I'm going to place at your feet my "common sense," my fear, my concern for myself. You've gone out of your way to take care of me. Therefore you deserve the gratitude of my trust. I trust you, Lord, and that trust is my sacrifice of praise. I will not worry about tomorrow when you've so graciously given me today.

Lord, you've raised me up, you won't let me fall now. You've made the sun shine and birds are singing and children come to play in front of my house. I won't worry because, I too, am a child of God. Today I'm going to your house to play gratefully in your shadow.

I'm sorry, though, that I can't share this moment with your other children. I've always wanted to offer a sacrificial meal to share with the poor who come to the Temple. But two copper coins won't buy much bread. Lord, I'd like to have others share my thanksgiving, to join with me in offering gratitude. I wish the whole world could know what you've done for me. I want everyone to know how wonderful you are.

Still, I know you know. This will be our secret, hm? You see and know my gratitude. You'll stand witness to the sacrifice! Besides, you know I won't keep still when the neighbors come over. I'll tell them what you've done. So you be prepared when they next come to you with prayers!

Sacrifice is such a special thing. It's my prayer made visible. I feel almost invisible with such a poor widow's mite. See me, Lord, and make my life an offering of gratitude and praise. Amen!

A Jericho Publican

"Maybe an angel had arranged for me to climb that tree...."

I knew they hated me. Anyway, I thought they hated me for doing my job. I wanted them to understand how hard it is for me sometimes. If only they had to deal with the Romans. That would give them a different perspective on my work, or so I thought. I knew they thought me a wicked man for consorting with the Romans and collecting taxes.

My attitude was, well, if I didn't do it, someone else would. Probably that someone else would make even greater demands on them, or so I thought. I believed that people thought of me only as a greedy little man. That was, after all, how I often thought of myself, when looking in the mirror, or sitting alone in the darkness.

Why did I go out among them then? I don't know. I probably should have known better. Going out is just asking for trouble. It's bad enough when I have official business, then I have soldiers around to protect me. But that morning I went out on my own. I knew it was risky, but I wanted to hear this rabbi.

You think it's silly. I kept arguing with myself about it, too. Why, if I had wanted to hear a prophet, I could have bought a scroll and read it to myself. I didn't have to go running about the streets of Jericho looking for an itinerant rabbi. I'm considered an important man in this town. After all, I'm senior tax collector in Jericho and a servant of the Emperor of Rome.

Yet, there I was, up a tree and out on a limb, like any one of a dozen of the street urchins. In the Name of the God of Israel, I had no idea what I was doing. I wonder if I had really gone out of my mind. I felt completely ridiculous, and more than a little embarrassed!

On the other hand, the tree climbing had been a splendid idea. I didn't have to put up with the crowds on the ground pushing and shoving in every direction.

I was safe from it all in that tree. Of course, I had to leave my robes on the ground. You can't climb a tree in a robe, any child can tell you that. I'd gotten the idea of tree climbing from the children, in fact. They knew how to get the best view of things.

It surprised me how friendly the children were towards me. I guess seeing a grown man climbing a tree made us companions for a while. They had no cause to resent my office, in that tree we were equals.

I asked this one curly-headed boy what he thought of this rabbi, Jesus? It took the lad so long to answer, I'd begun to think he'd lost his wits. Then I realized he was searching for someone in the crowd. He finally answered, "The rabbi is a prophet, sir, and God works miracles through him."

"Was it to see a miracle that you came out here?" I asked him this because I couldn't quite admit that this is just what I'd come hoping to see.

The boy pointed to a tired looking man who held a little girl. The mother, I supposed, was the woman fidgeting near by. The boy told me this was his family. The little girl was sick. The miracle he'd come to see wasn't some wondrous entertainment. It was a necessity.

You see, the boy quite innocently told me, they couldn't afford a physician. They had no money left for that. It seems they'd been forced to sell their land when the taxes were last increased. The boy had no way of knowing that I was the man who'd called for that increase. Since then, the father had been working as a day laborer in the fields of richer men. I wondered if he'd even worked on mine.

Maybe an angel had arranged for me to climb that tree so I might begin to see the world from a different perspective. I used to think poverty was only a result of laziness. I never realized that poverty would wear the face of a sick little girl with a mother and a father. I never thought of poverty as having a brother just my size.

Of course I knew people suffered with the taxes, but Caesar must be paid one way or another. But as I looked at the father's face, I began to wonder if my own house had to be so grand, my own coffers so full. Did my own fields need to be so large?

You know, I'd thought I could earn with my wealth the respect I could never command by my stature. But I recognized beneath me, one smaller than I, suffering to pay for my dignity. That struck me.

I began to ask myself some hard questions. What kind of dignity did I really have? I'd been half chased up that sycamore tree! Did people really hate me? Did they condemn me? I've been separated from my family, my people. I've been cut off from my heritage and I am as an alien to my God. I might as well be a leper. The deference people showed to me was the distance required by fear. Any hope for respect had fled from me.

Then I looked around me and saw the crowds. They were all gathered here to meet one man, a rabbi. The stories I'd heard about him said he was poor, a simple man. People flocked to him lavishing love and respect. Yet, I've never heard anyone say whether he was tall or short, lean or fat, fair or ruddy or any such thing. I've heard it said that he is strong, loving and wise. I'd heard it said that he scolds and chides, and laughs and embraces. I'd heard reports of how he could weep and dance. His stories seem both simple and profound. The tales told of his miracles indicate that they are never done for show, but for some kind of healing.

What struck me most of all, was this, the family right below me, had come today placing all their hopes in him. This alone made me reconsider what is meant by dignity and respect.

I was so busy with these thoughts that I hadn't noticed the crowds beginning to move. The babbling increased as the people moved down the street. Then I began to panic. I had no idea how to recognize the rabbi. One of these men is Jesus, I thought, but I had no idea which one. There was no halo, no panoply, no giant among men, no prophetic voice calling out. Which one, I asked, which one?

I had begun to believe that I'd been sitting here all day for nothing. I had come so close, and still would not have seen him. When suddenly the crowd came to a standstill and there below me were two dark eyes shining with friendliness. I really didn't quite hear his words, the crowd was rumbling so. It was something about needing a place to stay. He was inviting himself to my house to rest.

Can you imagine? Jesus! My house! Me. Yes, "Yes," I cried. I slid down the tree in my hurry, I could hardly wait to reach him. But as I touched the earth I could hear the mutterings of the crowd. They told him I'm the sinner, the greedy little tax collector, the Roman collaborator. They told him. I couldn't argue, it was true, after all.

But when I raised my head and looked him in the eye, he didn't seem to hear what they were saying about me at all. It seemed as if he saw a different me, the me I'd come to see, the frightened lonely person, ashamed of my size, confused about my life. He understood all that, and still he came to me. He wasn't coming to the house of a tax collector, but the crowd didn't know that. Jesus was coming to the house of a sick child in need of a miracle of healing.

That's when I looked around to see the face of the tired man with the little girl tight in the circle of his arms. They had been crucial in my cure and I owed them something for that.

I truly believe that I owe them my salvation, but how do you pay for that? I still don't know. But I began by giving half my possessions to the poor, beginning with them. The price of a physician begins the restitution for what I've done. I looked at Jesus and wondered, "Do you understand?"

He then put his arm around my shoulder and told me a story about fathers and sons and reminded me once again, that I too am a child of Abraham.

The Woman
and the
Well

"...I was in no mood to wait on some man at the well. I'd had enough of men for one morning..."

Isn't that just like a man? Want! Bring! Fetch! Carry! Woman, give me a drink. Nothing to do but sit by the well and wait for some woman to come along with a bucket and a rope. Nothing to do but think of promises and smiles. Don't I know? And you're right, I'd never learned to say no.

I'd planned to say no. When I woke up that morning with that donkey driver snoring and pawing me in his sleep, I promised myself I would learn to say no. You can believe I was in no mood to wait on some man at the well. I'd had enough of men for one morning, I didn't want to bother with another one and I was looking for an excuse to tell him so.

Then he smiled at me. Nothing's worse than having someone smile at you when you're in a bad mood. And I was in one of my worst. And there he was, smiling! Not leering, not laughing at me, just smiling, like a child smiles when it wants to make friends. You know, smiling with his eyes wide open. Not just looking at me, but seeing me. It felt funny, so I smiled back.

That's when I knew my bad mood had been ruined. You can't really smile in a bad mood, and I really smiled.

Then he asked me for a drink. Of course, I thought, he wants something. But he was still smiling, wide eyed. So I drew up some water and handed it to him. He put it down. It was eerie. He didn't even take a sip. I couldn't figure out what he was up to.

He sat back down and reached out his hand. I took it. He tugged at my hand, lightly, and motioned for me to sit with him. So I sat. Then he let go of my hand, pulled the bucket over to him and told me he thought I looked thirsty. I told him he was crazy. He said he'd been told that before now.

He asked me to tell him something about myself. What was there to say? I told him that I was a pretty boring subject. Then he laughed and said he'd never been bored and wouldn't mind seeing what it was like. So I started to tell him. I told him about the donkey driver and my new resolution about learning to say no.

He looked at me for a while and then he said I deserved to say no. He said that if I could learn to say no, my saying yes would matter more. I told him I didn't matter much anyhow. He said I mattered to him. I asked him who he thought he was that I should matter to him. He laughed again. Then he said I'd better pay attention, he might even be the messiah waiting here for his angels to gather. That's when I laughed. We both laughed. And it felt good.

We got into some pretty serious talking then. I think we talked over just about everything I'd ever done. I kept saying it was nothing, he kept telling me how it mattered. Somewhere in all the rememberings, or maybe it was in his caring, something opened up for me. I began to recognize that I did matter. I mattered to me. My saying yes or no mattered to me. I knew it. I was thirsty with wanting to do for myself. And I told him so. And you know what? He got up, went over to the well and got me a drink.

I laughed at his simpleness. He smiled with his wide eyes. Then he told me that I didn't have to be thirsty. He said I had a well deep inside, and it was full to the brim with mattering. All I had to do was take the lid off.

I just stared at him. The puzzlement must have been plain on my face. He got real serious. Then he said God doesn't live up on the mountain, or in the Temple. God, he said, is Spirit, and that Spirit rises in me like water in a well.

And if I listen to that Spirit, and want what she wants in me, then I'm being true to myself. And if I learn to live like that, everything I do will matter. He said that's the only worship God wants. Then his eyes got twinkles and said that's all the messiah wants, too. We both laughed. Then I reached for the bucket.

I don't know for sure that I'll never be thirsty, but I've come to believe that, deep down inside, I'll never be dry.

Zebedee's Wife

"Can't you hear the people around you who think you're all crazy? Or worse, the ones who claim you're dangerous?"

So, your friends gave you a hard time did they? Well, I'm sorry. I'm sorry if I embarrassed you, overstepped a mother's place. But, was it too much to ask? I wasn't asking for myself. And, if you want to know, I wasn't asking for you either. Have you even looked at your father lately? I was asking for him.

Your father was born to be a fisherman, as his father was before him. As we thought you would be after him. Boats, nets, winds and market prices. Day in and day out we lived these things. It's what your father loved. All he ever talked about was fishing. And you. Two strong sons to make a father proud. You both took to the water like fish. Your father always said you had seawater for blood. You were born fishermen, hauling in a catch with the best of them.

I should have seen it coming. Andrew bar Jonah taking you off to that baptizer. Then that man came from Nazareth and off you go as disciples of a rabbi. You're going to be fishers of men. I should have known the sons of Jonah would get you into trouble. Simon is so hotheaded.

You should have seen your father when he came home that day. A great catch you'd all made. He said that both boats were filled almost to the verge of sinking. And all it cost him was his sons. You should have seen his face! He said you just ran off with not even a blessing asked or given. Old Jonah tried to comfort him. Simon had a family, after all. He'd bring you all home when you came to your senses. But Zebedee knew better, and so did I.

My sons, sons of thunder, both of you. When you make up your minds there's no arguing with you. You left Zebedee sitting in the boat with only the hired men to help him. He knew you wouldn't take up the nets again. Now he hardly has the heart to take them up himself.

Whenever your rabbi returns to Capernaum your father just sits at home and watches the door. I knew that something had changed when three days ago he told me he wanted to sell the boat. I knew he'd given up waiting. Can't you see? It's not the fishing or the boat he's giving up. It's you. He's stopped hoping for a future, a way to carry on as a family. And you don't even see the hardest part of this. We don't understand what this is that we've given you to.

You follow a rabbi who speaks of kingdoms, then pays his taxes. He heals and performs great miracles and then asks them to be kept secret. Some call him the messiah, but even the priests don't believe in him. How will he convince the Romans? You follow him, but where is he leading you? Your father's sacrificed so much, are we really losing you?

James, you keep promising glory. John's head is full of angels and fire. You brag about the demons who flee at your command. Can't you hear the people around you who think you're all crazy? Or worse, the ones who claim you're dangerous? While you dream of holy kingdoms, I have nightmares about a Roman cross. What you're doing frightens me! Can this rabbi and his kingdom be worth all this?

I thought of Zebedee, and yes, I did think of you. If this rabbi really is to be king, then what does he offer you in his kingdom? He must know what you've given up. Does he know what we've given up? What does he promise in return?

Was it really too much to ask? A little reassurance you would have a place at his hand? A little consolation that Zebedee would have a legacy, was it too much to ask?

Don't you find comfort in the answer he gave me? True, he wouldn't promise you places at his side, but he offered to let you drink from his cup. Isn't it an honor to share the royal cup? Isn't it a privilege to drink with the king? Even Zebedee smiled when I told him about it. He could imagine just how it would look. Wasn't it worth a little teasing to know it? Surely, it wasn't too much to ask.

Still, I wonder, maybe you can tell me? Why was your rabbi so sad when he answered? Didn't he think a share in his cup would be enough?

A Friend

"Father, is my hour really here?"

Father, Lazarus is my brother. I love him. There are so many who surround me, who call me, who want me to do for them. Lazarus has always wanted to do for me. Lazarus has loved me too.

But, Lazarus is dead. Or is he? I don't want Lazarus to be dead. I want him to be only sleeping, not dead.

Father, do I have the right? Do I have the power and the right to use it to make death die? Do I have the right to call back the dead, to say "Rise"? Do I have the right to choose to use it on a friend? It was different in Naim, with the widow's son. I raised him for her. I raised him for the people, and to give you glory.

But, Father, I want to bring Lazarus back for me. I want to know him alive again. I want to see him, to touch him, to speak with him, here and now, on this side of life. But do I have the right?

Father, how can I know, for certain? My motives are mixed this time. I can't lie to you about it. I can't afford to fool myself.

I know there is a risk with the Pharisees. I know the mood of the people in Jerusalem. I know the Romans won't stand for much more.

This could be the beginning of something that will consume me in the end. Father, is my hour really here? Dare I ask Lazarus to come back to spend the hour with me?

Dare I ask Lazarus to come back? Would that really be best for him? For his sisters? Or even for me?

Father, do you have a will in this? Then let me do it! Just let me know it. Let me have some sense of what will make the most sense in the end. I know I have the power, or anyway I think I do. No. I know I do.

Doubting isn't a reason to let this choice pass me by. Doubting isn't a reason. That's the answer after all, isn't it?

I can't begin by doubting that I've known you all along. I can't doubt that I've listened to you, and that I've acted and trusted in you, all along. I've had to trust the themes and patterns that have played all through my life. I've trusted the words and images that I've prayed through all my life.

I've trusted you to back me when my passions led me into ways my understanding scarcely understood. I've trusted that my instincts, my insights have been good. And I've been willing to follow them through.

Father, this will be a miracle. His sisters will be consoled. My followers will be aroused. The Sanhedrin will be confused and the Romans will be concerned. It will set a precedent. It will raise more questions about life and death and after-life, whatever that's supposed to mean.

But, Father, there will also be Lazarus. Right now, that's answer enough for me.

Amen.

Martha

on

Mary

*"I mend the tunics
and wash the linen.
Mary sits at the feet
and pours the
ointment out."*

You just had to know my sister, that's all I can say. If you knew Mary as I know Mary, nothing would surprise you. You think she was extravagant with the nard? Let me tell you, Mary was extravagant with life! She has to be the freest woman I've ever met. She's also the most scatterbrained.

Mary is one of those people you have to tell to come in out of the rain. When we go out in the evening I still take two shawls along because Mary forgets that it gets cool after sunset.

When we were girls together you could always tell her handiwork from mine. Hers was the spinning with the broken threads, hers the uneven weave, and her sewing had the crooked seams. And her cooking made her sewing look good.

Her household talents never improved. She's one of those women who can't seem to get water to boil. Her boiled eggs were either so soft they could still be hatched, or so hard you could bounce them over the roof. God forbid she should roast the meat! She would always manage to forget the spit, which allowed the guests to choose between raw meat or burnt. Her method for baking was to overheat an oven so that the crust would blacken quickly with a doughy center as a dinner surprise.

Believe me, if I ever asked for Mary's help in the kitchen, I had to be pretty desperate.

Ah, you've heard that story. Yes, the Master could be nourished by the food of holy conversation, but his disciples were looking for supper. They were a ravenous crowd, and such a lot of them.

Yes, Mary had chosen the better portion. Of course she had. She always did. But John took the hint and came over and lent a hand with the milk and the cheese, and the plate of fish.

You see, Mary has a gift. She has a listening soul. It's as if her ears went straight to her heart. Her eyes would get wide, her face would light up, and her heart would wrap itself around the feet of the one who spoke to her. I don't mean to say this only happened with Jesus either. Mary listened this way to everyone.

Mary's gift is that she not only hears, she really understands. She could always understand the baby noises of children too young to talk. She has an uncanny way of understanding even the sounds of animals, too.

And she still has a way of listening to the most tongue-tied or taciturn men in Judea! Mary listens to their hearts with her heart. And I swear she seldom bothers to involve her head. Something which has caused her no end of trouble.

When she was younger, Mary would bring home every hungry waif, every stray animal and every broken-hearted man that came along. I took charge of the waifs, Lazarus would tend the animals, but Mary would fuss over the men.

You may have heard that at one time my sister was thought of as a loose woman. Well, Mary was never loose, but she was, perhaps, a bit too extravagant. She would get carried away whenever she stumbled across a hurting soul. Mary would give them her attention, and her consolation. She gave in her own way, and that was always extravagantly.

You see, Mary has never been one to do things half way. It isn't in her. She's a passionate woman, and when she does something she really puts herself into it. She always gives her whole self.

It's been hard being the practical one all the time, but it comes from living a lifetime with Mary. Not that I'd want any of the heartache she's had to bear, the malicious tongue-wagging that continues even today. I've seen her cry from a broken promise. I've seen her used and discarded. I've seen her most precious gifts just thrown away.

But I've also seen her take the better portion, and seen how much better it is!

Don't get me wrong. I've complained enough about having to do all the preparations for a feast while she was entertaining all the guests. I've spent a whole week cleaning the house for a celebration, only to have the guests remember how Mary decorated the place with her smile. But please don't think I've been jealous. That's not what I mean.

You see, Mary never took advantage of me. She never tried to overshadow me. She never deliberately placed herself out front. It's just that I always found it so easy to step behind her.

I guess, I've always been a shy one. Practical Martha,

organized Martha, hard working Martha. Shy, quiet Martha. I managed to hide my shyness behind a cooking pot, or beside the loom. Mary learned to overcome her shyness by growing a listening heart. I showed others what I could do. Mary reflected to others who they could be.

Of course, I listened too. You can overhear much behind a cooking pot. Then in the space around the fire you can ponder what you've heard.

But I missed the smiles and the winking eyes because I kept my head bent over the kneading board. I wish, sometimes, that I'd had the nerve to sit like Mary, looking up, content just to be a listening heart for another.

Just listen to me ramble! You asked about the nard. Yes, the priceless nard. We'd bought it several years before. Lazarus bought it, as a wedding hope for one of us. I wrapped it up in carded wool and set it in a cool dark place to protect the jar and preserve the scent. We didn't know how long we'd want to keep it. You see, we didn't have any proposals at the time.

I, naturally, took charge of the nard. I didn't even know for sure if Mary had any idea where it was.

Did I mind her taking it? Yes and no. No, I didn't mind the way she used it! She poured it out on him. It was the best possible thing she could do. He'd given us back our brother so short a time before, and Lazarus is more precious to us than a tub full of nard. Besides, you know what happened to the Master afterwards. What better way to use the nard than as our gift to him?

No, what bothered me was that I didn't do it. I could have, the nard was mine, too. I know the Master would have accepted it from me. I could have done it, I was right there. But, I couldn't because I'm Martha, the practical one who doesn't do those things. I cook the fish and roast the lamb, pour the milk and cool the wine. I mend the tunics and wash the linen. Mary sits at the feet and pours the ointment out.

I envy that. But I don't believe I'd really want to change it, even if I could. I am who I am, and I know he loves me just this way.

Yes, he said that Mary chose the better portion, but he ate a double portion of my fish that night. He also said that my bread was every bit as good as his mother's. Is there any praise higher?

Yes, he promised that people would always remember Mary and the nard, but he remembers me. And that is quite enough.

Hosanna

"I only saw his back, and it was bent, as if it were burdened with the weight of the world."

Did you see him pass this way? So many people pushed ahead of me. I hardly saw the donkey's tail, and nothing of the prophet! I never saw so many people all in one place. Then more and more kept coming. Could you believe the noise? All that singing and yelling! The noise echoed from the city walls as if the stones themselves had started to shout. And the children! Did you seem them? As if the going up to Jerusalem wasn't exciting enough, here was an excuse to start the celebration early. The Songs of Ascent weren't even enough for them. Did you hear the Hosannas too?

What do you think it all means? Is this prophet from Galilee, this wandering rabbi, really the Messiah? He looked the part, didn't he? Complete with donkey's colt. But, couldn't anyone have read the prophets and know about riding humbly to Jerusalem, on the foal of an ass? I mean, is that really humility, or is it choosing to fulfill the prophecy? I can understand why the authorities are so divided over him! Is this rabbi just being smart? Or, is he being wise? Does he ride a donkey's foal so that we may believe in him? Or does he ride the colt because he knows we do believe in him?

Why, if he is about to be proclaimed Messiah in Jerusalem, and what else could this procession mean? Why, if he is to be proclaimed king by all these people, did his back look so burdened? I know I didn't see him very well. The crowd, the palm branches waving around him. Maybe he was smiling, even laughing. Maybe his face was giving a different message. I only saw his back, and it was bent, as if it were burdened with the weight of the world. Is being Messiah a burden then? I know there's Rome, and the High Priest. They can be a burden for us all. But the Messiah's going to save us from that burden, isn't he?

Is that it, then? Does he save us from the burden by taking it on himself? We're asking him to save us. Hosanna! Is there no way to save the Messiah from the weight of his burden? If not, why would anyone admit to being Messiah at all? It must be from God. If the work is so heavy and still this man is willing to carry it, then it must be from God.

I wonder if the donkey felt the weight of it all? Poor little fellow, so new to the work of carrying burdens. Does he know he carries the weight of Jerusalem on the shoulders of the Messiah? Does Jerusalem know it? Her burden is lifted and placed on the back of the man who hears the prayer, Hosanna. How will God answer that prayer?

How will you save us, rabbi? How will you lift this burden up to God? How will you fend off the Romans? Will you storm the Temple gates on a donkey's back? Will you bear a palm frond instead of a sword? Or, will you find another way? Perhaps you know a mercy seat from which to reign over your people. Can it be any rougher or less glorious than the back of an ass's foal?

If you are the Messiah, Prophet of Gallilee. If, someday you do become King of the Jews. If you find a way to balance that burden, then, rabbi, do remember me when you come into your kingdom.

It Is Finished

Was her son born to die like this? Or is this the way her son happened to die?

Standing there she waits and watches. The clouds have covered a blazing sun, bringing heaven close. If they thought to use a Roman cross to lift up her son, they could see how the sky bent down to meet him. The sky a pouting gray, barely holding back her tears. Don't bother holding back, drop down, heavens, and weep.

Did Sarah know what Abraham had in mind when he and Isaac went off to the mountain Moriah? Or do mothers ever know? Is this what he came for, to die? Like this? She doesn't understand! He preached a loving Father God, one you could picture with a child on his lap. He spoke of a God who loved Samaritan women, healed Gentile children, cured cripples on the Sabbath and, even, raised the dead.

If God cares even for the dead, then why does her son suffer and die? Like this?

He dies alone, or almost alone. Two thieves hang at his side. They don't even know him. They never walked with him. Why should they be his companions now? Where are his disciples? The crowds that once gathered and made the stones echo from calling his name, where are they? Why does he die away from them? Why does he die alone?

Because everyone dies alone. Death is always done alone, even in the presence of a crowd of witnesses. Dying is a lonely thing. It has nothing to do with the people left behind.

Suffering is different. Suffering can be shared. Passion can be companied. Compassion is its name. The cross that weighed his shoulders down, weighed equally on her heart. Loving asks at least that much. She stood fixed to that place beneath him just as firmly as he was nailed to the wood.

The blood that dripped from his hands and feet accompanied the tears that poured from her broken heart. He suffered so much to die like this. Loving God, couldn't he suffer just a little less? Or, only, not much longer? She would be willing to suffer more, if he could suffer less.

He should have stayed a carpenter! What a mockery for a carpenter to be tortured to death by nails and wood! If his father had only known. But then, his Father knew, or did he? Was her son born to die like this? Or is this the way her son happened to die?

Did God have other plans? Even other hopes? Is this ending by design or merely with permission? What is God's will? Does God take her son's life, or does God receive her son's life? Joseph stayed a carpenter. Joseph, too, had died. Taken or received?

She remembered a prophet, years ago, warning her heart about a sword. She remembered her son, not so long ago, trying on a prophet's robe that she had made. A soldier owned it now, a gambling prize. She remembered a promise, when she was a girl, to bear a love that would ask this much. Her promise of love, a vow. Had she taken it, or received? Into God's hands she had committed her spirit. Now she prayed God to receive an only son.

She watched his face as he breathed out his last. His body fell limp. The wind combed his hair. The clouds began to cry.

Sunday Morning Conversation:

Mary of Magdala said....

"…an angel told me this; and angels can't lie."

He is risen! The angel said so! John, you do believe me, don't you? Peter, it's what he said would happen. Mary, Mother, you must know in your heart it's true!

The angel said so. I couldn't have imagined it. You can be sure I know something of the spirit world. I walked around for many years with seven devils locked inside. I know the rustle of their wings and how your ears ring with their words. I can recognize an angel when I see one.

I know what you're thinking. "She's overwrought. It's just some fantasy of grief. It's just a passing fancy." Well, let me tell you. I know angels.

I paid a price to be able to recognize an angel – the terrible price of demons once owning me. Or maybe it's more true to say they conquered space within my soul, lived there deep inside. I heard them murmuring, their cries and shouts.

I fought them when they wanted to claw their way to the surface and sometimes I almost won. We wrestled and struggled and trembled together. I came to know them each and every one, down to their very depths and mine. Demons remember where they came from, and I can tell you, more than one of them would like to live as a messenger of light again. Believe me, I can recognize angels; an angel told me this; and angels can't lie.

Oh, I can understand your doubts. I felt them first, before I knew, before I recognized him standing there. You see, I thought he was the gardener until he called my name. When I raised my head and wiped my eyes, I knew it was him standing there. He spoke to me and sent me here to bring the news to you. It's the angel's news of Galilee and what we need to do.

All right. I can see you won't believe me. But if you won't believe then come and look and see for yourselves. You know where we laid him. The tomb is now a place where angels sit and speak of him. They say he is risen and has gone ahead to Galilee and that he'll meet us there.

Oh, you of little faith. You are so slow to believe. It makes you so slow to laugh. Why, what if he should walk right in? Be with us in this very room? Past bolted doors and latticed windows? He would transform the very air we breathe with the radiance of his presence. Would you even drop your doubts at the sight of him? Then would you trust an angel's word to me?

Why does it seem impossible to you? Resurrection's not unknown. Go talk to Lazarus and see. Then maybe you will begin to believe a mystery of living that overcomes the tomb.

I was once filled with devils and I hadn't even died. If Jesus could bring me back to life from that, why shouldn't he come back himself and give life to us all?

Jesus raised the dead, healed the sick, cast out demons and opened our eyes to love for each other. Is loving, then, so easy for you that the miracle of rising seems too hard to be believed? Perhaps you've never been dead enough to understand the power of his preaching. Perhaps if you had met a few more devils, an angel wouldn't seem so strange. I do believe in angels and in the miracles I've seen. And I believe that he is risen, because I know how I've been raised.

And John said...

"Yes, I know he raised up Lazarus, but Lazarus can't return the favor."

Mary, believe me, I know how you feel! Don't you think I want to believe what you're saying? Don't you know how much I want him to be alive, to be with us? God knows! I would give anything. I would give my life to make these last three days go away, as if they'd never happened. But they did happen.

I was there. I was right there beside you. I watched what they did to him. The Romans, the priests. I saw what we did to him. We were his friends and we deserted him. Yes, I was there. At a distance where it was safe. Sure, I stood beneath his cross. I stood beneath him because I didn't have the courage to hang there beside him. I was there and you know it. You know how much I wish that it had never happened, but it did.

Fantasies won't change it! This is the real world, Mary. A world with priests and Romans and sealed tombs. This isn't some magic kingdom with shiny angels and ghosts. You can't let yourself believe that sort of thing. It will only drive you mad. You have to deal with the realities. You have to deal with what really happened, even if you wish it hadn't happened at all.

Mary, stop it! Stop looking at the door as if you thought he'd walk right in. It isn't going to happen, not through that door anyway. That door is locked and barred, and so is he, behind a sealed tomb.

Yes, I know he raised up Lazarus, but Lazarus can't return the favor. Jesus was the one who raised the dead. But now he's dead himself. Life is dead. Don't you understand? The Lord of life is dead. The world is dead but doesn't know it yet. The end has come to all the dreams, but we can't wake up and see it.

Mary, please don't carry on. Can't you see the pain you're causing? It isn't faith you're asking of us. You're asking us to forget the cross and wash the blood from our eyes. I can't do it. I, for one, just can't do it. The cross and blood are all I have to remember just how far love is willing to go. I can't pretend that his love wasn't unto death. And if death isn't what happened, then why did he seem to die at all? He was never a cheap magician doing miracles to thrill the crowd. Mary, don't you think if he could rise from the dead, he could have found a way to come down from the cross? He could have come down and saved himself, and us. He didn't have to suffer like that. He could have saved us all the grief. This grief is just too much to bear.

Don't look at me like that. Don't flash those big brown eyes at me. You stand there telling children's tales of angels and of glowing light. Mary! Don't you realize, the gardener was only a gardener after all? What will it take to prove it to you? What will it take to make you give up this fantasy and see the truth?

All right. I know what it'll take. I'll come with you to see the tomb. I'll even help you roll back the stone, if the guards will let us near it. Maybe then, when you see him there, you'll know what reality is all about. But I wish there were another way. It takes more than just words with you. You'll have to see the body.

Are you coming, Peter?

And Peter said...

"That door is locked because of me."

Come? Me? Where? To the tomb? With guards and soldiers all about? How dare you even ask? If I wouldn't come to see him die, do you think I'll go to see him dead? How could I go? I'd only desecrate the tomb.

John, you're worse about this than she is! She wants you to believe that he isn't dead. You want me to believe that I'm not dead. I find her story more convincing. After all, I wasn't there beneath the cross. I didn't see the blood and tears. For all I know you all were wrong. Maybe he only slept awhile. Maybe he is alive. But I'm another story. I killed a friendship. I betrayed a friend. Denying him, behind his back. Denying him to save myself. Denying, as he prophesied, before the cock crowed twice.

That door is locked because of me. Because I need it locked to keep my enemies out, and my fear inside. Because I'm still afraid of Temple guards and soldiers and death on a Roman cross. What's the matter, John? Don't you believe that crosses lurk outside the door for those of us who followed him? No wonder you won't believe in resurrection, you won't believe in the possibility of your own cross!

And John, what if she isn't dreaming? What if all she says is true? What if he isn't dead? Then what are we going to do? Why hasn't he come here to us? Why did he appear to her? Do you think it's because we turned our backs? Because we weren't there to see him die, now he wants no part of us, a second time around?

But that's not true for you, is it? No. You were there beside the cross. You had the nerve, I'll say that for you, you showed yourself to be a friend of his. So maybe there's a chance he'll show himself to you. He always loved you best, you know. So go with her. Let him see you loved him just as much.

And John. If by chance the lady's right. I mean, if he is alive again, or living still, no matter how. John, ask him, please. Say for me... tell him that I heard the cock and I... John, just tell him that I'm here.

Mary,
the mother of Jesus,
said...

"He appeared inside my womb, didn't he? Why shouldn't he appear outside of his grave?"

John, Peter, go with her. Yes, both of you, go with her. Don't ask me why; just humor an old woman. If it makes you feel better, John, you can tell yourself that two witnesses will be more convincing for her. Peter, if it will make you happy, say it's because I'm concerned about the guards. Whatever you want to believe, I would just like the both of you to go with her. Please?

All morning I've had a feeling. Something's happening, somewhere. Mary may have the right of it.

I know that look! You think I'm just dreaming, too. You think I've latched onto any hope to have him back again. But that's not what I'm feeling! Call it woman's intuition. If I didn't believe him dead would I have left him in the tomb? I saw him die, you know that, John. I heard him breathe his last. I even held him in my arms. You saw me. But something is different somewhere and I want you all to go.

If only I weren't so old, or only not so slow, if only it wasn't such a long walk from here, I'd tag along. But this is a trip for faster feet. So go on. I'll wait back here for you.

Trust me, Peter, I'll be all right. I'll lock the door behind you. I won't let any strangers in.

What's the matter, John? Don't be silly. I'm not encouraging her. You forget, I've seen an angel once or twice and she's right about the rustle, almost a whisper in their wings. And watch what you say about gardeners. He gardened with me in Nazareth when he wasn't in the carpenter shop with his father. Who knows, Peter, he may even appear as a locksmith before the day is done.

Don't look so surprised. Of course I believe her! He appeared inside my womb, didn't he? Why shouldn't he appear outside of his grave? God will be God in the end, you know.

Now look what you've done with your reluctance to go. You've got an old woman preaching at you. No doubt, you think she's a grief-stricken old woman, too.

Will you stop staring at your feet and start moving through the door? Go! Test Mary's words, and test these feelings in my heart. Go and see the place where we laid him. Go! And, send back word to me. Is the cross the limit of love, or do angels herald more?

With Prayer

I do not believe that the life of Jesus of Nazareth, the Christ, was meant to be merely a book tour. He sought followers, not admirers or fans. His invitation was not to an idle entertainment but into a life of transformation – transformation of self and, by the inevitable effect that holy people have on the world around them, transformation of the entire created universe.

The Gospels of Matthew, Mark, Luke and John record a ministry of healing and peace, of self-sacrifice which leads to the only true and lasting wholeness. The New Testament accounts of early Christian communities let us glimpse the beginnings of the human struggle, still going on, to accept Jesus' invitation to follow him.

These stories *are* intended to hold your interest, but like the canonical Gospels, they are also intended to engage far more of the reader than merely the imagination. The following questions are intended to invite you into the Bible stories from which they are inspired and into the Spirit which still calls each of us into a change of heart. Be brave, answer fearlessly.

147

The Innkeeper's Wife

Luke 2:1-20

1) Is there any busy-ness in my life that keeps me from being aware of Christ in my world?

2) What keeps me from stargazing, or even earthgazing?

3) Do I take the daily miracles of life for granted?

4) Is there a cave, an inner darkness that might house God being born?

5) How might God be birthed in the darknesses of our world?

Home Coming

Matthew 4:1-11; Mark 1:12-13;

Luke 4:1-13

1) Do I give credence to my own intuitions?

2) Have I dared to allow them to lead me to God?

3) Do I ponder as I move through life?

4) Do I tend to rush mystery?

5) How do I deal with immanent majesty, the divine that encounters me daily?

6) How do I deal with prophets? Ancient and modern?

7) What love have I been asked to bear?

Woman Healed

Matthew 9:20-22; Mark 5:25-34;

Luke 8:43-48.

1) Have I ever given up hope almost?

2) What kept me going?

3) Who or what touched me?

4) Have I ever experienced my center of creativity, my power, to be a source of suffering?

5) How have I been healed?

6) How might I still need to be healed?

7) Do I have a truth that God wants me to speak?

Talitha Cumi

Mathew 9:23-26; Mark 5:35-43;

Luke 8:49-56.

1) Have I ever been close to death, physically or emotionally, or even spiritually?

2) What brought me back to life?

3) What has fed me, nourished my life?

4) What have I hungered for, yet never tasted? Or haven't had for a long time?

5) What do I hunger for now?

6) How do I nourish others? Who or what have I fed?

7) Hoe do I replenish the world around me?

The Adulterous Woman

John 8:1-11

1) How have I experienced religion as a tool for oppression?

2) How have I experienced religion as liberation?

3) Who has been freed by my witness? Who has been condemned by it?

4) What kind of neighbor would I be to the adulteress? Even if she is myself?

5) Can I understand even when I don't approve? Do I? What does that mean?

6) What would have been written in the sand for me? For our culture?

7) In what way do I participate in these cultural sins?

8) Can I think of any sin that can really be committed alone?

She Who Loved Much

Luke 7:36-50

1) How do I experience being welcomed by others? By life? By all creation?

2) How do I welcome them?

3) To what or whom do I offer hospitality?

4) To what or whom do I refuse hospitality?

5) What or whom do I simply neglect?

6) What does love mean, today?

7) What is the emptiness in my life right now? How might I fill it? Does it really need to be filled right now, or would it be better to allow the emptiness to be there?

The Widow of Naim

Luke 7:11-15

1) Have I ever been in such pain that I doubted the blessing of life?

2) Who or what have I lost?

3) How do I deal with grief? What helped/helps me most?

4) How do I help others grieve?

5) How did I learn to let go?

6) How do I practice letting go, now?

7) Have I been able to be angry with God? How did he take it?

The Widow's Mite

Mark 12:41-44. Luke 21:1-4.

1) What is the difference between real common sense and fear?

2) Have I ever confused them? How do I tell them apart?

3) Have I ever sacrificed my fear or doubt? When and how?

4) How has God gone out of the way to care for me?

5) When did I last play gratefully in God's presence? With whom did I play?

6) How is my life an offering of gratitude and praise?

7) For what am I truly grateful?

A Jericho Publican

Luke 19:1-10.

1) What oppresses me? In what ways am I made to feel less than a blessing?

2) What have I done with that feeling? Have I become a healer or another oppressor?

3) What are my prejudices?

4) How might I turn them around?

5) Have I ever been up a tree or out on a limb? Why? How did I get there?

6) How did I come down?

7) How do I recognize Christ?

The Woman and the Well

John 4:5-26.

1) Have I learned to say no?

2) Do I say yes when I mean yes and no when I mean no?

3) Can I be really honest about my needs?

4) Do I really believe I count? Do I matter to me?

5) Do I really believe I matter to God?

6) How do I make a difference in the universe?

7) How does my inner well refresh others?

Zebedee's Wife

Matthew 20:20-23

1) Are there people in my life I don't understand? Who are they?

2) Are there situations in my life I don't understand? What are they?

3) What am I doing to increase and deepen my understanding?

4) What am I willing to give up in order to understand? Am I willing to change my mind? My values? My beliefs?

5) What do I feel insecure about?

6) What reassurance have I asked from God? Have I been reassured? Should I be?

7) The mother of James and John asked specific gifts for her sons when she really wanted assurance and consolation for herself. How do I try to get the right answers with the wrong questions?

A Friend

John 11:1-44

1) When do I doubt my own power?

2) When do I doubt God's power to work through me?

3) Who or what would I want returned to me: How can I reclaim that gift or relationship now?

4) What are the themes and patterns in my life?

5) How can I recognize them?

6) Do I trust them? How has God used them?

7) What are the greater patterns that shape our lives as a people?

Martha on Mary

The story of the better portion is found in Luke 10:38-42.

The story of the nard is found in Matthew 26:6-13. Mark 14:3-9. John 12:1-8.

1) How am I Martha?

2) How am I Mary?

3) What in my life has been like the nard? What have I done with it?

4) When have I not poured out the nard? What prevented/prevents me?

5) When have I poured it out? How did I do it?

6) How has my nard been received?

7) Anointing was used to heal in ancient times. What wounds do I desire to anoint in myself? In those close to me? In the world around me?

Hosanna

Matthew 21:1-9; Mark 11:1-11;

Luke 19:28-38; John 12:12-16.

1) What are the burdens of our world today?

2) How do I personally add to them?

3) How do I help shoulder them?

4) When do I really notice their weight?

5) How does that weight bear me down?

6) How can I make Christ's Kingdom real?

7) Do I remember to live in that Kingdom?

It is Finished

Matthew 27:31-60. Mark 15:15-46.

Luke 23:33-54. John 19:17-42.

1) How have I experienced being alone? Especially in my suffering?

2) Have I ever been companioned in my suffering? How?

3) Who wept for me? Who wept with me?

4) How have I experienced suffering with another?

5) What crosses have I stood beneath?

6) How have I experienced dying in my own journey?

7) How do I experience the dying of the world?

Sunday Morning Conversation

Matthew 28:1-10. Mark 16:1-11.

Luke 24:1-11. John 20:1-18

1) How have I been raised?

2) What devils have I known? When have I met angels? Who were they?

3) What have I locked out of my life?

4) What have I tried to lock in?

5) What lurking crosses am I afraid of?

6) What dangers am I willing to face for an encounter with life?

7) How is God being God in my life? In my world?